Churches
of Pakistan

Dr. Safdar Ali Shah
Syed Javaid A. Kazi

CP
CONSTELLATION Plus

Text
Dr. Safdar Ali Shah

Photography
Syed Javaid A. Kazi, Hon, EFIAP, MFIAP, FRPS, FPSA, MUSPAi

Valuable Contribution of Photographs
Aftab Ahmad, EFIAP, ARPS, FPSA
Syed Jaffar R. Gardezi
Syed Fakhar Zaman Azer, Uncle Tony
Obaid Samuel Bhatti
Yasir Nisar

ISBN 978-969-9532-00-9

Published by
Mansoor Rashid
info@constellationplus.com
+92 300 5142 051

Design and Production
TOPICAL Lahore Pakistan
info@topicalprinters.com
Printing: Speed Master CD 74 Heidelberg

Contents

Quaid's Commitment to Minorities

... Minorities to whichever community they may belong will be safeguarded. Their religion or faith or belief will be secure. There will be no interference of any kind with their freedom of worship. They will have their protection with regard to their religion, faith, their life, their culture. They will be, in all respects, the citizens of Pakistan without any distinction of caste or creed **....**

—Muhammad Ali Jinnah
The Founder and First Governor General of Pakistan
14 July 1947

The State shall safeguard the legitimate rights and interests of minorities, including their due representation in the Federal and Provincial services.

—Part II: Chapter 2: Principles of Policy – [Article 36]
The Constitution of Pakistan

Preface

More than religious buildings, the churches symbolize the spirit of a community and cultural context of centuries. Whereas the churches built during the colonial period were invariably inspired by the European architectural traditions, the new churches manifest local ethos and modern outlook. The beautiful new churches in the federal capital, Islamabad, are distinctive and representative of the new trends in local architecture. Our Lady of Fatima Church, consecrated in 1978, stands out for its modern architecture which signifies a fresh outlook of the local Christian community, in harmony with the cosmopolitan culture of Islamabad, besides its name—Fatima is a revered name in the Islamic tradition as the name of the beloved daughter of the Holy Prophet (Peace be upon him). It was designed by a Muslim architect. St. Thomas Church, consecrated in 1990, is the newest addition to the churches in the federal

capital. It bears the stamp of indigenous architecture with a modern perspective. All Saints' Church in Peshawar (Khyber Pakhtunkhwa) is more of a Christian "mosque" than a typical church, which makes it unique. The Persian calligraphy at the main entrance adds to its oriental ambience. The Cathedral of the Most Holy Redeemer in Multan blends with the architectural harmony of the Sufi shrines in the city, lately renovated with the traditional glazed tiles from Multan. Likewise, the Cathedral of Faisalabad is a magnificent religious edifice; so is the Cathedral of Lahore which is designed as an eastern church. These are not isolated buildings; they represent the local parishes and the vibrant Christian communities nearby. The older churches on the other hand are archives of colonial history, meticulously preserved by the church authorities.

There are hundreds of beautiful churches all over the country. They are all sacred edifices in terms of their function and the passion with which they were built. Owing to space limitation, it was difficult to cover all the churches in this book. We have selected more representative structures, irrespective of their religious denominations. The purpose is to showcase the architectural beauty and variety of church edifices in Pakistan; our heartfelt apologies to those parishes that could not be accommodated.

"Churches of Pakistan" has been a fascinating subject in many ways. From its very inception, the concept educed avid approval and unreserved support from everyone, especially church authorities, intellectuals, community leaders and my Christian friends. Without their assistance and good offices the work would not have materialized. In particular, I would like to acknowledge with utmost gratitude the wholehearted help and facilitation of church authorities who allowed our camera crew into the precincts of holy churches. The local priests were courteous and helpful which made the job easier—our sincere thanks to them all. I would also like to record my gratitude to the prime mover and the publisher, Mr. Mansoor Rashid, the CEO of Constellation Plus, who translated a dream into reality;

Mr. Ahmed Salim, Presidential Pride of Performance, who shared his research work on minorities and lent expert advice; Syed Javaid A. Kazi, Presidential Pride of Performance, the photographer, who travelled tirelessly to capture the architectural beauty and spirit of the churches; Mr. Mehboob Sada (late), Director Christian Study Centre; Mr. Robinson Asghar for their valuable support and assistance. Mr. Ashir Moeen, the coordinator, who bridged many a barrier to meet the planned timelines. It was a team effort and every member's contribution counted and is fully acknowledged.

I hope these pictures do justice to the beautiful buildings that they attempt to portray.

Dr. Safdar Ali Shah
December 2010
Islamabad

An early image of the All Saints Church in Peshawar. This majestic edifice, built by the British in Mughal style, beautifully blends with the historical buildings in the city.

HISTORY OF THE CHURCH IN PAKISTAN

Churches in Pakistan are not only an inescapable feature of the landscape of our major cities and towns; they elegantly portray the religious diversity and well-being of our vibrant Christian minority. Their distinctive architecture attracts the locals and tourists alike. They are not just the beautiful buildings, they are an important part of our cultural history, mostly well preserved and documented. They tell the story of the colonial rulers and the Christians in this part of the world. The new churches show a happy blend of modern and indigenous trends and stand in harmony with the surroundings like the communities who share a common history, a common culture and collective aspirations as Pakistanis.

Apostolic Origin

Christianity arrived in the subcontinent almost the same time as it reached Europe. It is traced back to the middle of 1st century AD when, according to a tradition, Thomas the Apostle came to this part of the world. Thus, he is credited with the founding of Christianity in the subcontinent.[1] He is believed to have come to Andrapolis (present-day Taxila, near Islamabad) and converted the King Gundafor.[2] He then left for southern India where there was a Jewish population in the coastal areas.[3] During his missionary journey, he reached Mylapore on the east coast near Madras, around 52 AD, where he is said to have converted the wife and son of a local king but was later killed— "pierced through with spears" on a hillside by the Brahmins.[4]

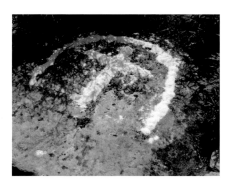

Supposed site of Apostle's footprint in Taxila.

Even if we may find it hard to confirm the tradition of apostolic origin of Christianity in Pakistan,[5] there is compelling evidence of the presence of Christians at various locations in the subcontinent during early parts of the first millennium. Discovery of crosses,[6] especially Thomas crosses, and the accounts of travelers make a coherent account of the advent and growth of the new faith in this region.

Early Christians

Eusebius, a church historian, reports of the presence of Christian communities in the third century in the provinces of the North-Chilas (now in Pakistan), which is reinforced by the discovery of Nestorian crosses at Gilgit and Chilas.[7] One of the delegates at the famous Council of Nicaea, held in 325 AD, under the authority of Emperor Constantine, called Johanne (John), endorsed his name as "Metropolitan (chief bishop) of Persia and Great India," which shows that there was an organized Christian community here in the 4th century.

The Thomas Cross discovered at Taxila.

Apart from Nestorian Christians, there was a presence of Armenians who migrated to India from areas under the Persian Empire. They flourished because of their knowledge of Persian which was the court language of the Muslim rulers. Many Armenian Christians distinguished themselves and held important positions in the Mughal court.[8]

Advent of the Portuguese

Vasco de Gama reached Calicut in May 1498. It was the beginning of maritime presence of the Portuguese in the Indian Ocean. They were fired with colonial ambitions and trade interests. Very soon they dominated the sea lines and maritime trade. They were followed by Franciscan Friars and Jesuit missionaries. The Friars built monasteries and churches but were not very successful at conversions. The Jesuits met with success but their converts were mainly from the lower castes.

Early Missionaries

A number of Catholic religious orders emerged in Europe during the medieval times and even later, which had proper Papal sanction and support, especially for missionary work. These were mainly Friars and non-Friars. The Friars included the Augustinians, the Carmelites, the Dominicans and the Franciscans (Capuchins and Friars Minors) – some of them are still active in Pakistan. The non-friars were the Jesuits or the Fathers of the College of St. Paul. They distinguished themselves during the Mughal Empire and gained access to the Mughal court and non-Indian Christian merchants and soldiers of fortune employed by the local rulers and princes. They led three missions to the Mughal court (1580, 1591 and 1595).[9] They were warmly received at the court and given a residence nearby. The king also attended their service. Mughal Emperors Akbar and Jehangir, known for their religious toleration, took keen interest in their affairs and teachings. On receipt of reports of such royal treatment of the Jesuits, Bishop Clement VIII wrote a letter of thanks and appreciation to the King in 1592.[10]

The Jesuits gained concessions from the Mughals and a written decree in 1602 allowing "freedom to worship, right to preach publicly and to make converts".[11] Jehangir also gave them land for a graveyard and even funds for building the churches. Strong Christian communities also emerged at Thatta and Lehri Bandar (in Pakistan) when these locations developed as trading stations. Two Christian groups were active during the Mughal times— Armenian merchants and soldiers of fortune. The growth of Christianity during the Mughal era had a checkered history; it fluctuated with political conditions and policies of the local rulers and the royal court. Missionaries were generally well treated by the Muslim rulers: "In 1708 there were five Missionaries in the interior. The Brahmans and Daseris, (heathen mendicant friars,) and other Hindoos, persecuted them; but they were protected by the Mahometan rulers."[12]

It is conjectured that there was a Christian presence in the Punjab up to the 7th century under the authority of Riv-Ardushir of Persia.[13] However, the first church on this land was built by the Jesuits on 27 September 1597. It was located near the Mughal court and the governor of Lahore personally attended its opening, for which musicians and musical instruments were brought from Goa. There were around one hundred Christians in Lahore in 1606 which rose to one thousand in 1614.[14]

British East India Company and the Protestants

The officials of the British East India Company were mainly Protestants but there were almost 50% Catholics in the rank and file.[15] As the number of Europeans increased, there was a need of chaplains with the regiments, especially due to rising number of deaths in military campaigns and tropical diseases. Before falling to the British in 1661, Bombay was a Portuguese station with 6,000 Catholics in a population of 15,000.[16] The Portuguese had an organized cadre of missionaries, on the contrary, East India Company did not allow missionaries in its territories. Being a commercial enterprise, "its Directors thought it bad to mix religion and business."[17] The new charter of the Company, passed in 1698, contained a clause that the Company should constantly maintain one minister "in every garrison and superior factory". As a result, there were as many as 19 chaplains at the beginning of the 18th century—one for each factory. However, it took them 80 long years to build the first Protestant church in a factory at Madras.[18]

The first Protestant mission was established in 1700 by the Dutch "Society for the Propagation of the Gospel in Foreign Parts". Thereafter, the church followed the march of the Company into the new territories. In 1850, there were as many as 309 churches, 17,356 members and 103,154 Protestant Christians, in India.[19]

The Railways

Railways played an important role in the promotion of Christianity. Interestingly, against a popular perception of strategic considerations, promoters of the new section connecting Karachi presented it as a philanthropic service. "Railways were to be employed to extend the benefits of enlightened western, Christian civilization to the most remote of India's benighted masses. The railway train would serve as a swift, safe transport for Christian missionaries, bearing the glad tidings of their gospel to eagerly impatient Indian ears."[20] However, the Railways helped establish Christian communities at all major stations as a large number of new converts and Anglo-Indians were absorbed in the expanding Railway network. It made them economically stable and independent and opened the door to new professions. Thus, it marked the emergence of first indigenous Christian communities, with a higher social status.

Post-Independence (1947) Era

The areas included in Pakistan were the last to be annexed by the East India Company – Sindh in 1843 and the Punjab in 1849. These areas, however, were not unfamiliar with Europeans or Christians. There were a number of foreigners in Ranjit Singh's Army, including more than 40 European officers. The Jesuit missionaries had visited the court of Ranjit Singh also, but there was no organized Christian community in the Punjab. Likewise, despite earlier presence of Christians during the Mughal days in Thatta and Lehri Bandar, there were fewer Christians in Sindh at the time of its annexation in 1843. Interestingly, there was a priest in Karachi in 1841, two years before the formal occupation of Sindh; and a French secular priest in the Punjab in 1846, three years before its annexation in 1849. He built a small wooden chapel in Lahore in 1847.[21]

Christianity formally came into Sindh and the Punjab on the heels of the East Indian Company. Thereafter, there was a rapid inflow of British forces along with missionaries. The earliest settlements emerged in

the cantonments and the areas nearby, especially in the Punjab. Chaplains were brought in to meet the spiritual needs of the Christian newcomers and their families. Sisters of Jesus and Mary arrived in 1856 and established their first school in Sialkot. St. Patrick School was set up in Karachi in 1861 by the Sisters of the Cross. A large number of missionary schools and colleges were founded during the second half of the 19th century which played an important role in the education of local population. In fact, there was no system of public education before the advent of the British. The colonists established government and aided schools which provided secular education. It was in the 1880s that Lahore was given an independent status of a diocese. A Vicariate was created in 1887 and Kashmir and northern areas were placed under the care of Mill Hill Fathers.

Another significant development was the establishment of Christian villages and farm colonies to group together scattered individual Christian families. The first Christian village was founded by Robert Clark in 1867 (now Clarkabad near Lahore). Mariamabad (Punjab) was established on 667 acres of farmland in 1893 which is a flourishing Christian community and home to the National Marian Shrine in the country. Other farm colonies like Khushpore and Francisabad (Punjab) came up later which played an important role in the growth of the Christian community in the rural Punjab. Over the period, six Catholic dioceses have emerged: Lahore, 1886; Multan, 1939; Rawalpindi, 1947; Karachi, 1948; Hyderabad, 1958 and Faisalabad, 1960.

The United Church of Pakistan was established in 1970 as a union of four denominations: Anglican, Methodist, Lutheran and Presbyterian (Scottish). Initially, it was organized into four dioceses: Karachi, Multan, Lahore and Sialkot. In 1980, four new dioceses were created: Hyderabad, Raiwind, Faisalabad and Peshawar. In addition to the eight bishops, there is a bishop for the Gulf Ministries. The presiding bishop, known as the Moderator, is appointed for a three-year term.

Minorities in Pakistan

Pakistan was created primarily to safeguard the interest and identity of the Muslim minority in a Hindu-dominated India. Therefore, the founding father, Muhammad Ali Jinnah, was fully mindful of the status of minorities in the projected state of Pakistan. When asked to make a statement on minorities in a press conference in New Delhi, a month before the creation of Pakistan, Mr. Jinnah said:

> . . . Let me tell you that I shall not depart from what I said repeatedly with regard to the minorities. Every time I spoke about the minorities I meant what I said and what I said I

meant. Minorities to whichever community they may belong will be safeguarded. Their religion or faith or belief will be secure. There will be no interference of any kind with their freedom of worship. They will have their protection with regard to their religion, faith, their life, their culture. They will be, in all respects, the citizens of Pakistan without any distinction of caste or creed. They will have their rights and privileges and no doubt along with this goes the obligations of citizenship. Therefore, the minorities have their responsibilities also, and they will play their part in the affairs of this state. As long as the minorities are loyal to the state and owe true allegiance, and as long as I have any power, they need have no apprehension of any kind.[22]

He reiterated his commitment and articulated his vision of a democratic Pakistan before the Constituent Assembly a month after the creation of Pakistan:

If you change your past and work together in a spirit that everyone of you, no matter to what community he belongs, no matter what relations he had with you in the past, no matter what is his colour, caste or creed, is first, second and last a citizen of this State with equal rights, privileges, and obligations, there will be no end to the progress you will make. . . in course of time, Hindus would cease to be Hindus and Muslims would cease to be Muslims, not in the religious sense, because that is the personal faith of each individual, but in the political sense as citizens of the State.[23]

His vision and commitment is now enshrined in the Constitution under the following provisions in the Preamble:[24]

Wherein adequate provision shall be made for the minorities freely to profess and practice their religions and develop their cultures;

Wherein adequate provisions shall be made to safeguard the legitimate interests of minorities and backward and depressed classes; . . .

Rights of the minorities have been fully protected and safeguarded through the Fundamental Rights in the Constitution,[25] such as security of person, safeguards as to arrest and detention, prohibition of slavery, forced labour, etc., inviolability of dignity of man, etc., freedom of movement, freedom of assembly, freedom of association, freedom of trade, business and profession, freedom of speech, freedom to profess religion and to manage religious institutions, safeguard against taxation for purposes of any particular religion, safeguards as to educational institutions in respect of religion, etc., provision as to property, protection of property rights, equality of citizens, non-discrimination in respect of access to public places, safeguard against discrimination in service and preservation of language, script and culture.

In addition to these fundamental rights, Article 36 of the Constitution states that "The State shall safeguard the legitimate rights and interests of minorities, including their due representation in the Federal and provincial services."[26]

Contribution of Christians in Pakistan

The contribution of Christians goes back to the making of Pakistan when they made a principled decision to support the All India Muslim League in the Punjab. All India Christian League and All India Christian Association, Punjab openly supported the Muslim League in 1945-46 elections, contested on the basis of Pakistan. They were ardent supporters of the Quaid-i-Azam in the Punjab. Later, the Joint Christian Board, an umbrella organization representing All India Christian League, Punjab, All India Christian Association, Punjab, All India Anglo-Indian Association Punjab and Catholic Association, met on June 21, 1947 under the leadership of Diwan Bahadur S. P. Singha, the last speaker of the Pre-Independence Punjab Assembly, (He was also the first speaker of the Post-Independence Punjab Assembly). They unanimously decided

to vote for Pakistan on June 23, 1947. It was a deliberate decision based on sound political reasons.[27] The local Christian members not only polled three crucial votes in favour of Pakistan but the Speaker made it a point to register his "casting" vote in favour of the resolution.[28] Not only that, they put their full weight behind the Muslim League during their representation before the Boundary Commission.

Although only about two percent of the total population, yet the Christian scholars, teachers, doctors, civil servants, social workers and lawyers have been active participants in the national life—from politics to armed forces, and civil service to judiciary. They played and are still playing an important role in social development of the country. Their role is acknowledged and appreciated. They were pioneers in many areas. However, their landmark contribution has been in the field of education and healthcare. The United Christian Hospital, where Dr. Bomes performed the first open-heart surgery in 1965, the Memorial Christian Hospital, Sialkot, the Holy Family Hospital, Rawalpindi, and many more, like the Leprosy hospital of Dr. Ruth Pfau, set new standards in healthcare. A large number of educational institutions were founded by the missionaries, and a number of them are still being managed by the church. There are iconic figures like Mr Catchpole (Education), Brigadier C. H. B. Rodham, SQA, CBE, DSO, MC (known as "father of sports"), Joshua Fazaluddin (Literature), F. E. Chaudhry (Photo Journalism), Ms. Mala, Saleem Raza (Music), and many more.

Christian officers have distinguished themselves in the armed forces, both during war and in peace time. The war heroes and decorated soldiers like Cecil Chaudhry, Nazir Latif, Shams Gordon, Anthony Chaudhry, Peter O'Reilly, Mervyn Middlecoat etc., are household names. At this point of time, the Dean and Director of Studies in the Pakistan Military Academy (Brigadier General) and General Officer Commanding of one of the field formations are Christian officers, besides many more retired two and one-star generals. A distinguished Christian lawyer is judge of the High Court in the footsteps of the respected Justice A. R. Cornelius, a former Chief Justice of Supreme Court of Pakistan and C. M. Lobo, the ex-Chief Judge of the Sindh High Court. The list of such luminaries is exhaustive. Moreover, a large number of Pakistanis are the product of missionary schools and fondly remember their teachers, mostly Fathers and Sisters, with terms of endearment and respect.

Communal Harmony

Muslim–Christian relations in Pakistan have always been cordial. At the time of independence, there was unrest and bloodshed around Anarkali in Lahore but during these riots and charged agitations, the Church and the orphanage remained safe.[29] During communal riots in other places, the properties marked with crosses stayed untouched. There are reported cases of Hindus escaping or being smuggled in Christian robes. The Fathers of Mill Hill who had established the Burn Hall School in Srinagar, moved to Abbottabad, Pakistan, after Independence, by choice.

Pakistan is a land of saints and sufis who preached amity, peace and universal love. Their teachings promoted religious co-existence, communal harmony and tolerance in the society. There have been isolated incidents of communal strife which are mere aberrations and should be viewed as such. What is important is the state policy and attitude of the civil society which have always denounced such incidents with full-throated condemnation. Similarly, some government decisions, like nationalization of missionary colleges have been reviewed. Moreover, organized efforts are underway to ensure the rights of minorities as equal citizens of the state as per the commitment of the father of the nation at the time of Independence (August 14, 1947).

Church Architecture*

Pakistan has a rich variety of architectural styles—from medieval to modern. The churches built during the colonial time generally followed the Western traditions because the European sponsors wanted to recreate the structures as part of their experience back home. However, the indigenous church asserted itself more vigorously which found an expression in the church buildings as well. The new churches manifest departure from European style and greater influence of Mughal and local architecture as seen in mosques, mausoleums and shrines. Despite all this, it is important to know the salient features of Western styles so as to appreciate the beautiful structures they inspired in Pakistan.

The Beginning

During the period of persecution, Christianity was "illegal" in the Roman Empire. After the conversion of Constantine and Edict of Milan (313 AD), "Christianity became the privileged religion of the Roman Empire". Emperor Theodosius (379-398) made it the state religion. It was then that Christians sought physical manifestation in buildings to glorify the name of God. It started with Basilica (from Roman basilica or hall of justice), a large east-west rectangular hall, with altar at the east end.† Gradually, it became more defined with emerging needs of the faithful and new rites being introduced. As the church became clericalised, the Two-room Church became the norm in Europe. The first room, called the nave, was used by the congregation; the second room, called the sanctuary, was the preserve of the clergy.

Medieval Period (1180–1275)

During the Middle Ages, the Roman Catholic Church dominated the life in Europe. Religion was a powerful factor which influenced church architecture. During this time, two distinctive styles of church buildings emerged. Both the styles manifest a strong desire to glorify God:

- The **Romanesque style** (450-1150 AD) developed all across Europe. The churches in this style were built in England after the Norman Conquest (1066 AD), and were called the Normans. They were massive structures, with thick walls, adorned by windows with semi-circular arches. The next development in Europe was the introduction of narrow, lancet window, often found in pairs or triplets. It was called the Early English or French style. It was simple and monastic in character with little carvings. The pointed arch and rib-vaults started to emerge under the influence of Islamic architecture especially after the capture of Toledo (1085).

- The medieval period marks the development of another distinctive style of church architecture called the Gothic style (1150-1500). It flourished during the high and late medieval period. It evolved from Romanesque architecture and was succeeded by Renaissance architecture. With the main structure based on the cross, it featured a pointed steeple directed towards the sky, a mark of religious aspiration and medieval faith. Its characteristic features include the pointed arches, the ribbed vault and the flying buttresses. In the later period, the walls became thinner, solid buttresses became more elegant, flying buttresses were surmounted by pinnacles; towers became taller and more decorated, windows occupied more and more of the wall space, decorative carving became more freely flowing and figures multiplied, particularly on the west fronts of cathedrals and abbeys. The introduction of steeple coincides with the Islamic influence in the Mediterranean region.

Reformation

The Reformation brought about a radical change in church design. The altar and tabernacle were often removed and replaced by a communion table and pulpit. Stone altar was replaced by a wood table. Catholic churches, however, retained their emphasis on symbolism. They added marble statues and gold fittings combined with superb stained glass rose windows.

The interiors of mediaeval churches, apart from their many altars and stained glass, had huge figures of the crucified Christ, high above the congregation, mounted on a rood loft at the chancel arch. A wooden rood screen beneath usually had painted figures of apostles and angels. While the Catholics built ornate churches with images and interior decorations, most of the Protestant denominations objected to images and insisted on simplicity in design and detail. King Henry VIII put an end to images and decorations. Edward VI had almost all of the internal decoration destroyed. Stone altars and images were smashed, glass broken, font covers and roods and their screens were torn down and burnt.

The Eastern Church

East and west began to diverge from each other from an early date. Whereas the Basilica, a long aisled hall with an apse at one end, was the most common form in the West, a more compact centralized style became predominant in the east. They copied pagan tombs and were roofed over by a dome which symbolized heaven. The centralized and Basilica structures were sometimes combined as in the church of Hagia Sophia in Constantinople (now Istanbul).

A variant form of the centralized church was developed in Russia and came to prominence in the sixteenth century. Here the dome was replaced by a much thinner and taller hipped or conical roof which, it is said, originated from the need to prevent snow from remaining on roofs. One of the finest examples of these tented churches is St. Basil's in Red Square in Moscow.

Renaissance Style

A new phase of church design, based upon classical culture, emerged with the Renaissance. The temples of pagan Rome became models for the new churches. Instead of having long vaulted naves and aisles, they had a centralized plan. Along with renewed interest in antiquity and art, the rise of theatre and opera provided another external source of ideas for the Church. There was emphasis on seeing. This, coupled with exotic Baroque, led to a new kind of church, providing distant vistas, with a scenic progression along the horizontal axis. The process reached the extreme in what is known as Rococo.

In the seventeenth century, a return was seen towards the single room church in which everything could be seen—altar and pulpit were both visible. The ideal was of an oblong building with a single space at the east end combining all liturgical acts.

Gothic Revival

The growth of big cities in the nineteenth century necessitated huge growth in church architecture. Buildings based upon classical models were dismissed as pagan. Instead, Gothic style was revived. Large churches, often much too large, were built in England, mostly according to some version of these ideas. The grandiose of these structures outshines the modest medieval counterparts. The style survived well into the 20th century.

Modernity

The idea that worship was a corporate activity and that the congregation should be in no way excluded from sight or participation is owed to the Liturgical Movement. Simple one-room plans reflect the essence of modernity in architecture.

A theological principle which resulted in change was the decree *Sacrosanctum Concilium* of the Second Vatican Council, issued in December 1963. This encouraged "active participation" by the faithful in the celebration of the liturgy by the people and required that new churches should be built with this in mind. It also encouraged the use of a freestanding altar allowing the priest to face the people.

Different principles and practical pressures produced other changes. Parish churches were inevitably built more modestly. Often shortage of finances, as well as a "market place" theology, suggested the building of multi-purpose churches, in which secular and sacred events might take place in the same space at different times.

Sources*

♦   http://en.wikipedia.org/wiki/Church_architecture
♦   P. Thomas, *Churches in India,* New Delhi: Reprint., 1990.
♦   Daniel Roselle, *A World History: A Cultural Approach*, Boston: Ginn and Company, 1963.
♦   Jean Bony, *French-Gothic Architecture of the 12th and 13th Century*, California: University of California Press, 1983.
†   It was mandated in the 10th century that the church would be so built that the nave pointed east so that the rising sun would shine on the altar, the faithful would "greet" the risen Christ, and the church would face Jerusalem.http://www.utccs.org/documents/churcharchitecture.pdf. According to P. Thomas, the church usually faced west so that the priest could perform the ritual facing east. P. Thomas, *Churches in India,* New Delhi: Reprint., 1990.

Notes and References

1   P. Thomas, *Churches in India,* New Delhi: Reprint., 1990, p. 1. Reportedly, there is a group of mystics in Thatta, Pakistan who trace their origin to St. Thomas. Fr. Lawrence Saldanha, *Hamari Dastaan (History of Catholic Church in Pakistan),* Lahore: Dar-ul-Kalaam, 1990, p. 16.

2   Gundafor (Gundaphorus, Gondophares, Gunduphara) is in fact a title held by many kings. According to archeological findings in the form of coins and a rock inscription at Takht Bahi (near Mardan, Pakistan), this particular Gundafor began to reign in 20 AD and was still reigning in 46 AD. "The story itself runs briefly as follows: At the division of the Apostles, India fell to the lot of Thomas, but he declared his inability to go, whereupon his Master Jesus appeared in a supernatural way to Abban, the envoy of Gundafor, an Indian king, and sold Thomas to him to be his slave and serve Gundafor as a carpenter. Then Abban and Thomas sailed away until they came to Andrapolis, where they landed and attended the marriage feast of the ruler's daughter." Thurston, Herbert, "St. Thomas the Apostle," *The Catholic Encyclopedia*, Vol. 14. New York: Robert Appleton Company, 1912. August 21, 2010 <http://www.newadvent.org/cathen/14658b.htm>.

3   P. Thomas, *Churches in India,* New Delhi: Reprint., 1990, p. 1.

4   Fr. Lawrence Saldanha, *Hamari Dastaan (History of Catholic Church in Pakistan),* Lahore: Dar-ul-Kalaam, 1990, p. 13. In fact, there are more than one traditions about his death, such as: He was killed by the Brahmins; was condemned to death and killed by soldiers; and that he was killed accidently by a low-caste Hindu, who was shooting at the peacocks, while the Apostle was praying on a hillside. The fact of the matter is that there is a granite bas relief on a hillside, with a Persian inscription, of around 6th century, which is believed to be the place where the Apostle laid down his life. It is known as Thomas Mountain.

5   There are skeptics like John Kaye who are in search of concrete evidence: "Slowly does reason reject a tradition which imagination is so eager to embrace. It would be pleasant to accord the fullest faith to the legend of the apostolic origin of Christianity in India but there is really no authority in its favour to divest it of all the attributes of fable." John William Kaye, *Christianity in India: An Historical Narrative*, London: Smith Elder and Co., 1859, p. 3. John Rooney terms it "a viable historical hypothesis" but also questions the authenticity of "Acts of Thomas" on which the tradition is generally based. See John Rooney, *Shadows in the Dark*, Rawalpindi: The Christian Study Centre, 1984, p. 46.

6   As many as five such crosses have been found in the subcontinent, including the one found in 1935 at an archaeological site near the city of Sirkap (Taxila), known as the Taxila Cross, which was handed over to the Christian community by the Government of Pakistan and is preserved as a sacred relic in the Church of Pakistan Cathedral at Lahore. The government has also allotted a piece of land at the site where Christians gather annually on the 3rd of July to celebrate the advent of Apostle Thomas at Taxila. Fr. Lawrence Saldanha, *Hamari Dastaan (History of Catholic Church in Pakistan),* Lahore: Dar-ul-Kalaam, 1990, p. 14, 15. Also see John Rooney, *Shadows in the Dark*, Rawalpindi: The Christian Study Centre, 1984, p. 44.

7   2006 Directory of *The Catholic Church in Pakistan*, Lahore: Renewal Centre, 2006, p. 20.

8   P. Thomas, *Churches of India*, p. 3. Some of them included Mirza Zulquarnain, under Jehangir, Gregory Khan under Mir Kassim, Khwajah Martinus, a merchant of Agra and Khwaja Safar of Madras, who beautified St. Thomas Mount in Mylapore.

9   Fr. Lawrence Saldanha, *Hamari Dastaan (History of Cathlic Church in Pakistan),* Lahore: Dar-ul-Kalaam, 1990, p. 18.

10   Ibid., p. 24.

11   John Rooney, *On Heels of Battle,* Rawalpindi: The Christian Study Centre, 1986, p. 49.

12   http://www.ebooksread.com/authors-eng/elijah-hoole/madras-mysore-and-the-south-of-india-ora-personal-narrative-of-a-mission-to--ala/

13   John Rooney, *On Heels of Battle,* Rawalpindi: The Christian Study Centre, 1986, p. 90.

14   Fr. Lawrence Saldanha, *Hamari Dastaan (History of Cathlic Church in Pakistan),* Lahore: Dar-ul-Kalaam, 1990, p. 19.

15   John Rooney, *On Heels of Battle,* Rawalpindi: The Christian Study Centre, 1986, p. 46.

16   Ibid. , p. 29.

17   P. Thomas, Churches in India, p. 5,6.

18   John William Kaye, *Christianity in India: An Historical Narrative*, London: Smith Elder and Co., 1859, p. 52.

19   John Rooney, *On Heels of Battle,* Rawalpindi: The Christian Study Centre, 1986, p. 90.

20   Ibid., p. 61.

21   Ibid., p. 43.

22   ---, *Jinnah - Speeches and Statements 1947-1949*, Karachi: Oxford University Press.

23   Mr. Jinnah's presidential address to the Constituent Assembly of Pakistan, August 11, 1947.

24   National Assembly of Pakistan, *The Constitution of the Islamic Republic of Pakistan*, 1993 ed. p. 1, 2.

25   Ibid., p. 7-17.

26   Ibid., p. 19.

27   Salamat Akhtar, *Tehreek-i-Pakistan Ke Gumnam Kirdar*, Rawalpindi: Christian Study Centre, 1997.

28   John Rooney, *On Heels of Battle,* Rawalpindi: The Christian Study Centre, 1986, p. 61.

Christ Church, Kotri (Sindh): This historical church was built in 1846 for the railway colony of the city. It is among the earliest churches of Pakistan. The congregation celebrated its 150th anniversary in 1996.

Our Lady of Fatima Church is among the new churches of the federal capital, Islamabad. Its distinctive design merges with the modern architecture of the city. This elegant edifice was designed by a Muslim architect, Anwar Said. The site of the church building was given to the Christian community by the Government of Pakistan, in September 1975, free of cost.

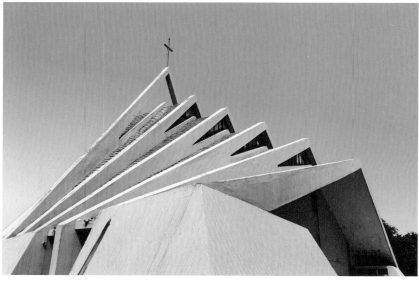

OUR LADY OF FATIMA CHURCH

Consecrated : 12th October 1979

Architect : Mr. Anwar Said

Contractor : MacDonald Layton Co. Ltd.

Funded by many benefactors,
especially Missio, Germany

Sanctuary Crucifix donated by
H. E. Mr. P. Angara-Aragon,
Ambassador of Philippines

Statue of our Lady donated by
H.E. Mr. F. Teixeira De Sanpayo,
Ambassador of Portugal

Crowning of Mary Festival at Our Lady of Fatima Church, Islamabad.

Built in local red bricks, St. Thomas Church was completed in 1992. It is located in a posh locality in the heart of the capital city, Islamabad.

St. Thomas Church, Islamabad: The ground breaking ceremony of this fascinating structure was performed by the Duke of Gloucester in October 1988, and the foundation stone was laid by the Archbishop of Canterbury, Dr. Robert Runcie, on February 3, 1990.

Different views of St. Thomas Church, Islamabad.

St. Paul's Church stands prominent on the Mall of Rawalpindi. It was built in 1908 for the local Garrison. The stained glass window in the rear of the church was installed in the memory of the English soldiers who fell during Momand Operation (Tribal Area) in 1920.

St. Mary's Church, Westridge, Rawalpindi was built in 1882.

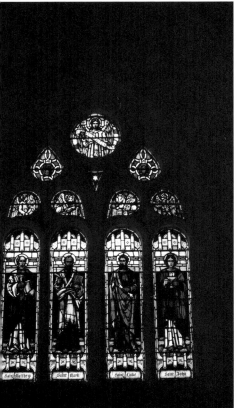

Interior of St. Paul's Church, Rawalpindi. Its stained glass windows carry images of the four authors of the gospels.

Christ Church was the first garrison church in Rawalpindi. Its foundation stone was laid on March 12, 1852. The church service started earlier in March 1851 in army tents. It was mandatory for the deputy commissioner, cantonment magistrates, the police and railway officials, soldiers and non-military residents to attend the church parade on Sundays.

Christ Church, Rawalpindi: The hammer beam roof is typical depiction of Gothic architecture. ▶

Wedding ceremony at the Christ Church, Rawalpindi.

Christmas celebrations at the Christ Church.

The Pro Church (Christ Church), Rawalpindi.

St. Joseph's Cathedral, Rawalpindi.

Interior view of the St. Joseph's Cathedral, Rawalpindi.

Holy Trinity Church with its 60-foot high tower stands prominent on the Mall of Murree, a hill station near Islamabad. It was opened on May 17, 1857. Queen Elizabeth II attended its service in 1997 during her visit to Pakistan.

HOLY TRINITY CHURCH
MURREE
FIRST OPENED   17TH MAY 1857
CONSECRATED   2ND MARCH 1860

The nave with the gallery.

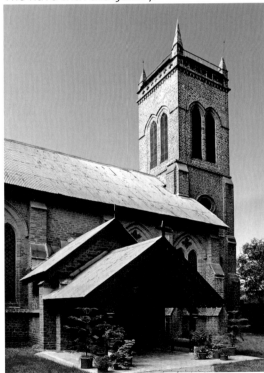

The entrance from the Mall.

The marble baptismal font.

Church of Seven Sorrows, Murree: The nave, the altar, the gallery and the hammer beam ceiling with hand carved wooden braces reflecting Neo-Gothic architecture.

St. Deny's Church, Murree.

West façade of the Church of Khanaspur.

150 years old manuscript of the Holy Bible and an old piano at St. John's Church, Jhelum.

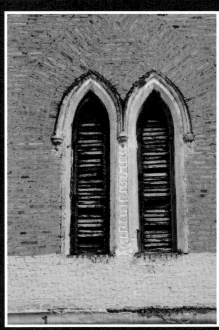

A beautiful specimen of architectural relief.

St. John's Church, Jhelum is located on the bank of the River Jhelum. The church is a unique combination of the Norman, Gothic and French architecture styles. This sturdy structure survived the massive earthquake of 2005.

Presbyterian Church, Jhelum.

St. Xaviour's Church, Gujrat, built in 1893, in early English style.

St. Andrew's Church, Gujrat.

St. Mathew's Church, Nathiagali: This century-old colourful wooden structure is set against the evergreen pines and cedars in a peaceful picturesque surrounding.

Built and decorated in Early English style, using pink sandstone, the Church Of Resurrection Cathedral, Lahore was consecrated on January 25, 1887. It has ten beautiful stained glass windows made by Leonard Walker from England. Its sacred treasure is crowned by the Thomas Cross, which was found at Taxila, near Islamabad and given to the Church by the Government of Pakistan.

The twin towers of the Church of Resurrection Cathedral, Lahore. The North tower houses the historic clock and the bell, manufactured in 1862. The bell case is still in use.

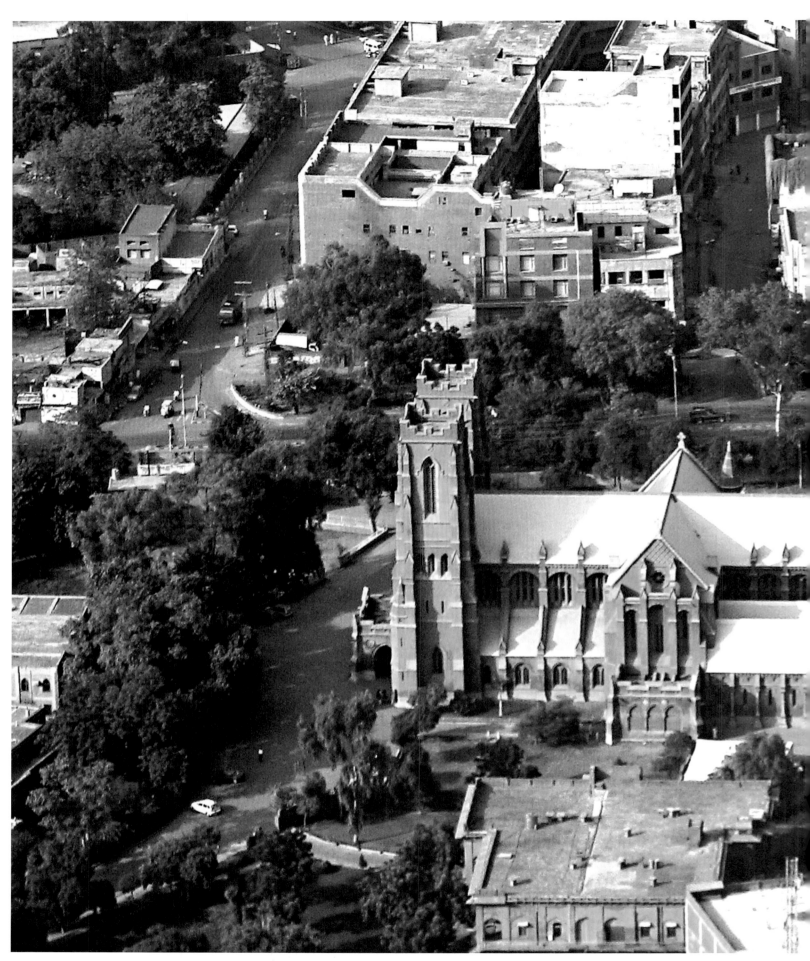

Aerial view of the Church of Resurrection Cathedral. Designed by John Oldrid, this superb structure stands prominent on the Mall of Lahore.

Church of Resurrection Cathedral, Lahore.

Aerial view of the Cathedral of the Sacred Heart of Jesus, Lahore with its lofty steeple, a massive dome and turrets. The Cathedral stands as a majestic monument in the heart of the city. It was consecrated on November 19, 1907 by Bishop Eestermans.

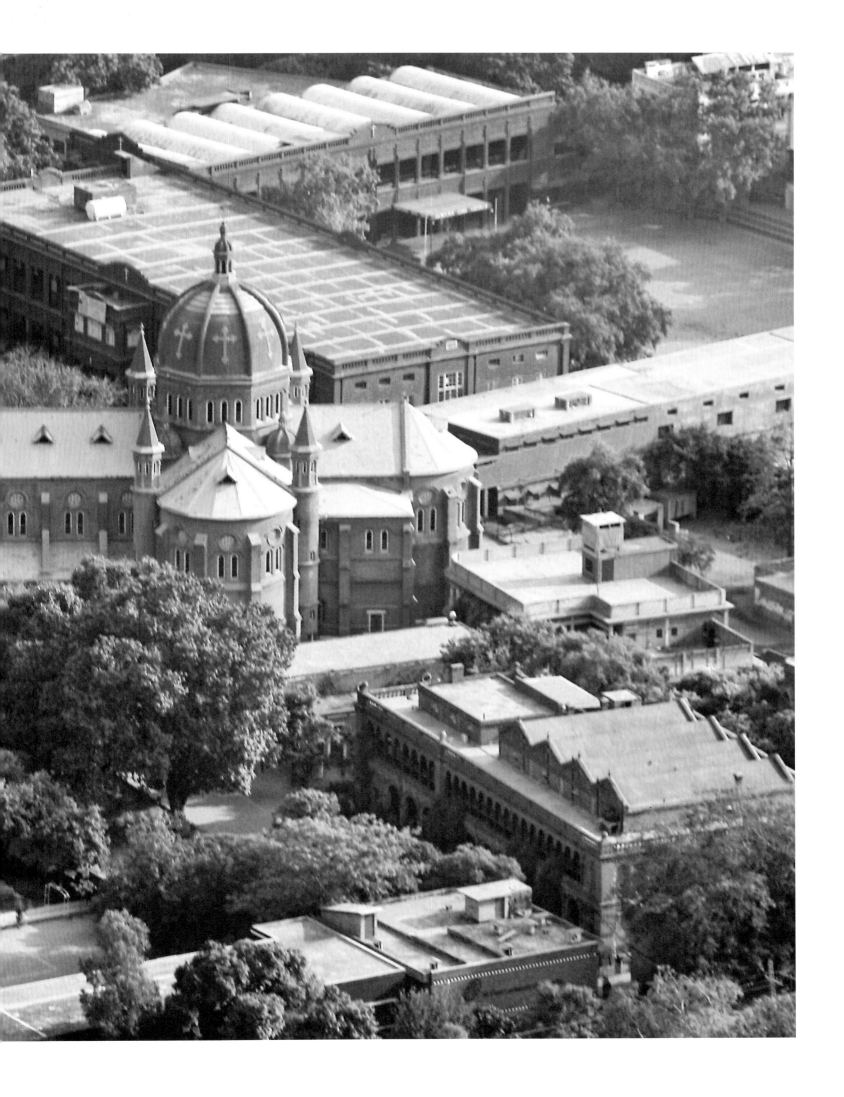

Cathedral of the Sacred Heart of Jesus, Lahore: Built in Roman Byzantine style, it was designed by M. Dubbeleere of Antwerp, a Belgian architect, for which he won the Prize of Rome. It is among the most beautiful churches of Pakistan. The belfry steeple is 165 feet high, the nave is 68 feet and the transept is 125 feet wide.

CATHEDRAL OF THE SACRED HEART OF JESUS

To The Glory of God

FOUNDATION STONE BLESSED

On 4. 10.1903

CONSECRATED

On 19. November 1907

The interior lit by ten stained glass windows.

The teak work entrance.

Sunday Mass.

The 120 foot high dome is supported by four elegant turrets.

Rib-vault ceiling with decorated stained glass windows and ornaments. A typical French-Gothic architecture.

The high altar with its delicately colored statues. The floor is made of white and grey Italian carara marble.

The west façade of the Cathedral of the Sacred Heart of Jesus, Lahore.

Interior view of the Cathedral of the Sacred Heart of Jesus, Lahore with its Gothic style rib vaulted ceiling.

Holy Trinity Church, Nila Gumbad, Lahore was built as a Cathedral for the local Christians during the British Raj.

Baptismal font.

The façade of Naulakha Church, Lahore.

St. Oswald's Church, Lahore was built for the railway employees in 1915. In 1965, it was handed over to the Church of England which later gave it to the Church of Pakistan.

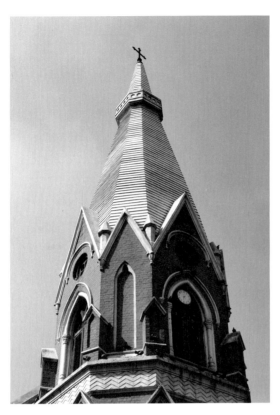

Different views of St. Anthony's Church.

St. Anthony's Church, Lahore, formerly known as "Railway Church" was consecrated in 1809. Expansion of the new Church wing was completed in 2007 with the help of donations from the local community. The steeple is inspired from French Gothic era.

St. Mary Magdalene's Church, Lahore was built by the British Army. Its foundation stone was laid in 1854 and consecrated in 1857. The entire building was colored in white to send out a message of peace, hope and love. The clock, called the "Godfather," was made in 1857 and it is still working.

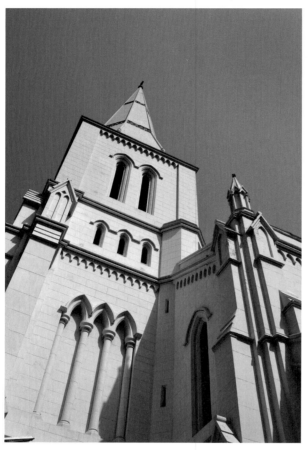

The tower is 150 feet high.

Painted stained glass window.

The marble entrance.

The gargoyle.

The floral structrue used at the vaults are made out of large piece of marble.

St. Patrick's Church, Sahiwal was
built by the British Army in 1865.
Till 1947, the Church service was
held in English only.

Sacred Heart Church, Sahiwal.

The Mount of Mary.

St. Peter's Church, Clarkabad Village (Punjab) was originally built in 1877 and consecrated on March 18, 1897. It was reconstructed and expanded in the year 2000, depicting local architectural style.

An interior view of St. Peter's Church, Clarkabad.

Exterior view of St. Peter's Church, Clarkabad.

◀ St. John's Church, Clarkabad Khurd (Punjab) was renovated in 1990 and reconsecrated on October 8, 1990.

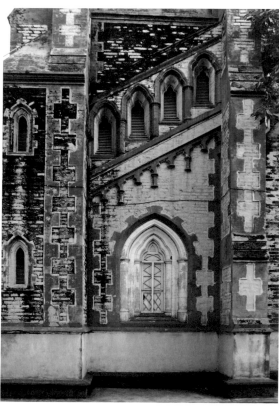

Hunter Memorial Church, Sialkot. It was built in 1861.

The façade of the Hunter Memorial Church, Sialkot. ▶

THIS CHURCH WAS DESIGNED AND
BUILT BY L.J.HARTLEY MAXWELL BENGAL ENGINEERS
THE FOUNDATION STONE WAS LAID ON 1ST MAY 1852.
THE CHURCH CONSECRATED ON 30TH JANY 1857.

SI MONUMENTUM REQUIRIS CIRCUMSPICE

Dais at the Holy Trinity Cathedral, Sialkot.

Holy Trinity Cathedral

◄ Holy Trinity Cathedral, Sialkot.

Epiphany Church, Narowal (Sialkot) was built in 1892 and consecrated on February 25, 1893.

The chalice used in the Holy Communion ceremony in the 1860's.

The cross was presented to the Church in 1936 by a local Raja Gambeer Singh.

The façade of the Jubilee Church, Sialkot.

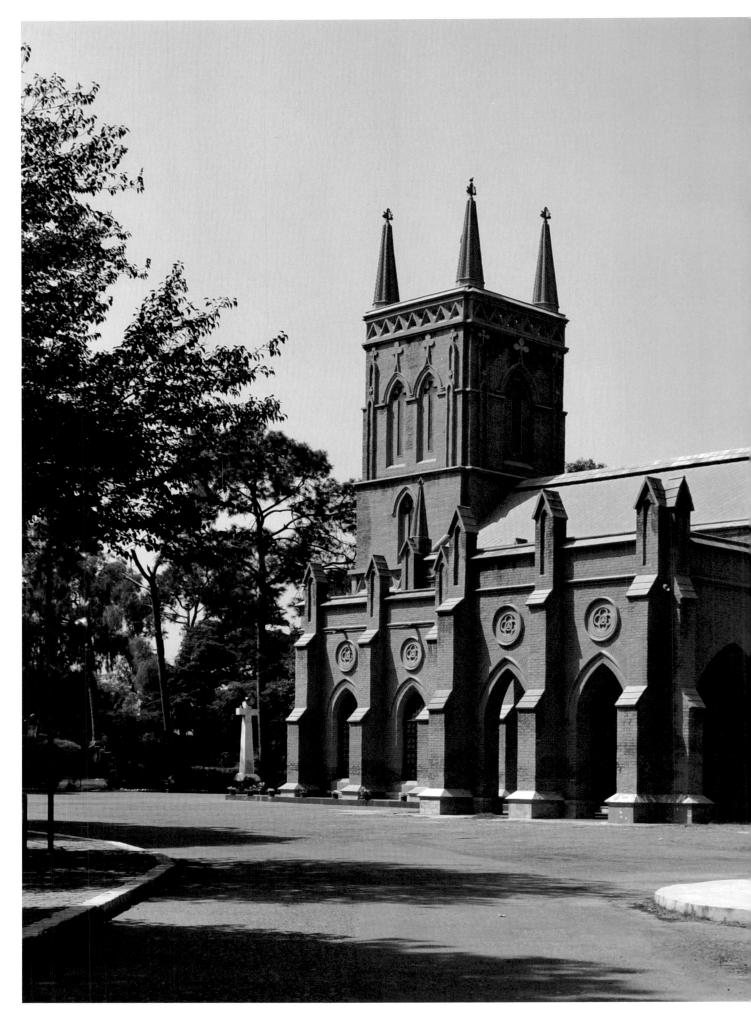

St. John's Cathedral, Peshawar.
It is 117 feet long and 68 feet wide, with a nave and two side aisles.

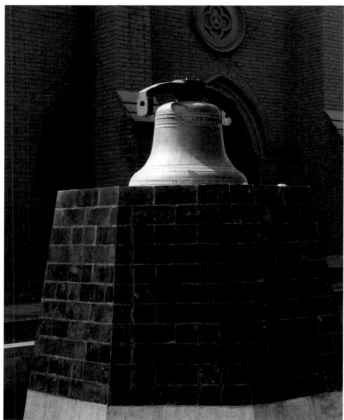

It was consecrated on February 1860. The Duke of Edenborough attended its service in 1960. Later, Queen Elizabeth II also prayed in here along with the Duke in 1961.

All Saints' Church, Peshwar (Khyber Pakhtunkhwa) is amongst the few churches facing Jerusalem.

All Saints' Church, Peshawar (Khyber Pakhtunkhwa - formerly known as North West Frontier Province) was consecrated on December 27, 1883. The Church resembles a mosque with Persian and Pashto verses from the Bible inscribed at the entrance. It blends with the mosques and minarets around.

Mission Hospital Chapel, Peshawar, built in 1904, resembles a mausoleum built in Mughal style, similar to the architecture of Hiran Minar, Sheikhupura.

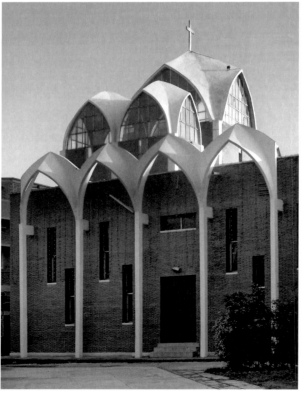

St. Michael's Church and Dervish Mosque on the Mall in Peshawar, Khyber Pakhtunkhwa.

Garrison Church, Risalpur. It was built in 1914 for the British troops and their families.

The skyline in Bannu, Khyber Pakhtunkhwa.

St. Luke's Church, Abbottabad was consecrated on October 18, 1865. The construction material is the same as that used by the Mughals in their buildings, such as lintel, lime and jute bags.

St. Peter & Paul's Cathedral, Faislabad—a fusion of modern, Italian and Pakistani architecture.

Chalice.

St. Peter & Paul's Cathedral, Faislabad.

Holy Rosary Church, Warispura, Faisalabad.

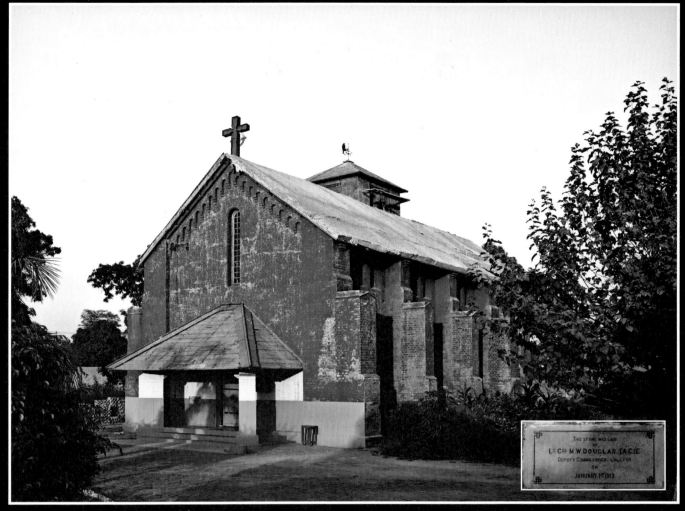

St. Peter's Church, Faisalabad.

Arooj-e-Mariam Church, Chak 7, Faisalabad.

Church at Chandra Ke, Gojra.

Sacred Heart Church, Gojra.

St. John's Church, Gojra (near Faisalabad), established on November 18, 1913.

Sunday Mass at St. John's Church, Gojra.

. John's Church, Gojra.

Church, at Chandra Ke, Gojra.

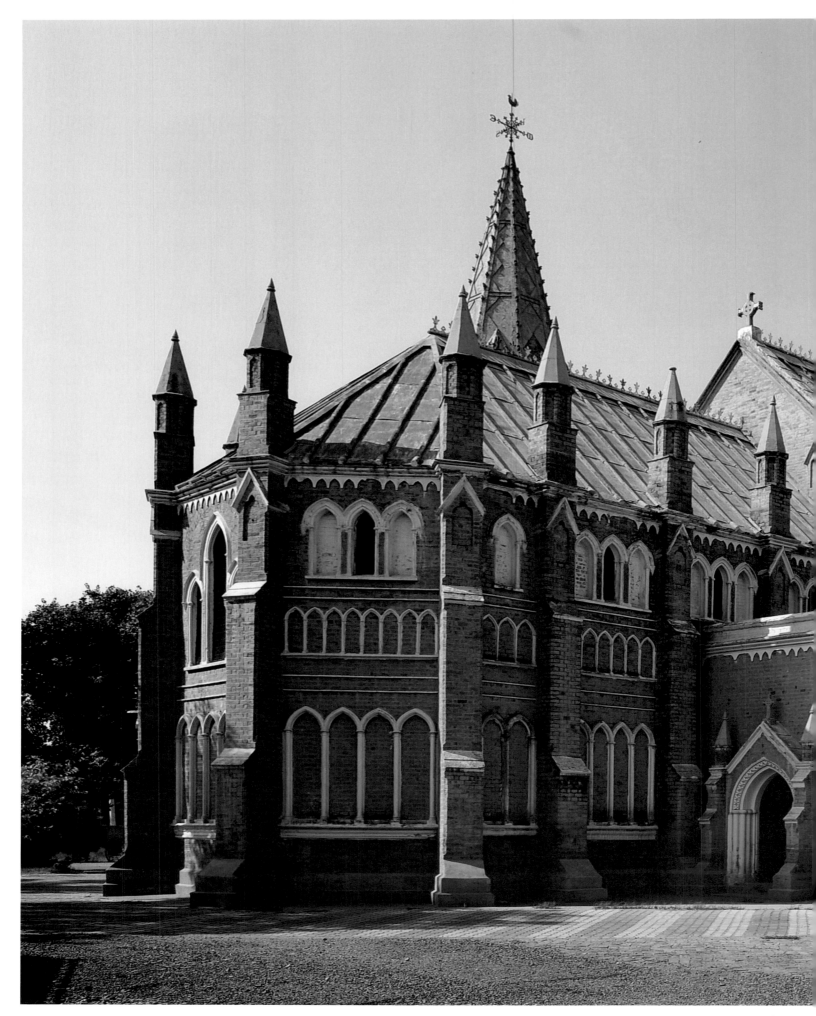

St. Mary's Cathedral, Multan, with its array of turrets.

St. Mary's Cathedral, Multan.

Jesus & Mary's Church and Convent School, Multan. ▶

Cathedral of the Most Holy Redeemer, Multan. The dome blends with the shrines of Multan, the city of Sufi saints. Its interior glitters with the local glazed tiles.

Crowning of Mary Festival at the newly built Uchrist Church
in a village near Mian Channu (Multan).

◀ The façade of St. John the Baptist De La Salle Church, Multan.

89

Bethel Memorial Methodist Church, Quetta, 1959.

Extension of Holy Rosary Church, Quetta.

Interior view of Holy Rosary Church, Quetta.

Located at the bank of the River Indus, St. Saviour's Church, Sukkur, is the second oldest church in Sindh. It was built in 1855 as a cantonment church for the British army and civilian officers.

The annual festival at St. Mary's Church, Sukkur, founded in 1886. The visitors are served with traditional dishes and delicacies on the occasion.

St. Francis Xavier Cathedral, Hyderabad.

Church of Reconciliation, Khipro, a desert town in Sindh.

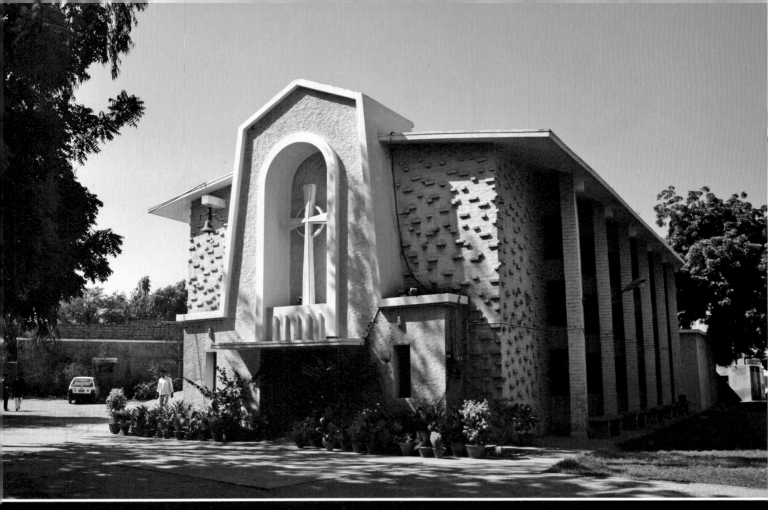

St. Philip's Church, Hyderabad was originally built in 1905. It was reconstructed in 1967 in a local architectural design.

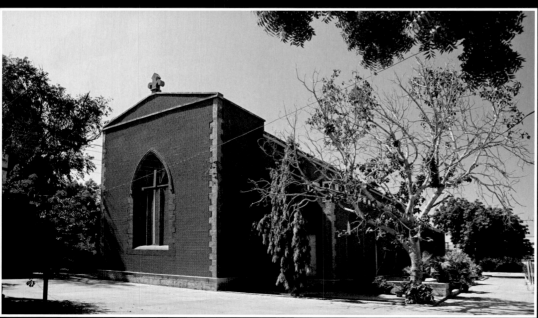

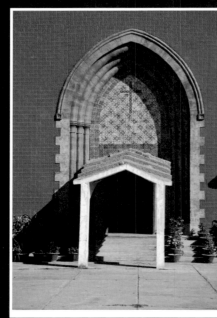

St. Thomas Cathedral, Hyderabad, was consecrated as a garrison church for the British army on February 26, 1860.

The altar.

A wedding ceremony in St. Thomas Cathedral, Hyderabad.

St. Patrick's Cathedral with its chapel in white marble and the school. The Cathedral is a majestic monument of the port city of Karachi. Its glorious edifice showcases the grandeur of the British Raj in its heydays. Established in 1878, the Church serves one of the oldest parishes of the country.

Romanesque architecture: St. Patrick's Cathedral, Karachi.

◀ The grand interior with ribbed vault and high stained glass windows in Gothic style.

St. Patrick's Cathedral, Karachi.

St. Andrew's Church, Karachi with its ten bays, flying buttresses and gabled windows is a typical Gothic structure.

St. Andrew's Church, Karachi is a cultural heritage building. Built in 1868, primarily to serve the Scottish community and named after St. Andrew, the patron saint of Scotland. The church is designed in the 14th century Gothic style with a 135 foot high spire and an octagonal porch by T. G. Newnhan, the resident engineer of "Scinde Railways." It stands as a symbol of binding connection between Sindh and Scotland.

St. Andrew's Church, Karachi with its attractive octagonal porch and the rose window.

St. Andrew's Church with a minaret of the local mosque in the background, signifying the religious harmony of the two communities in the city.

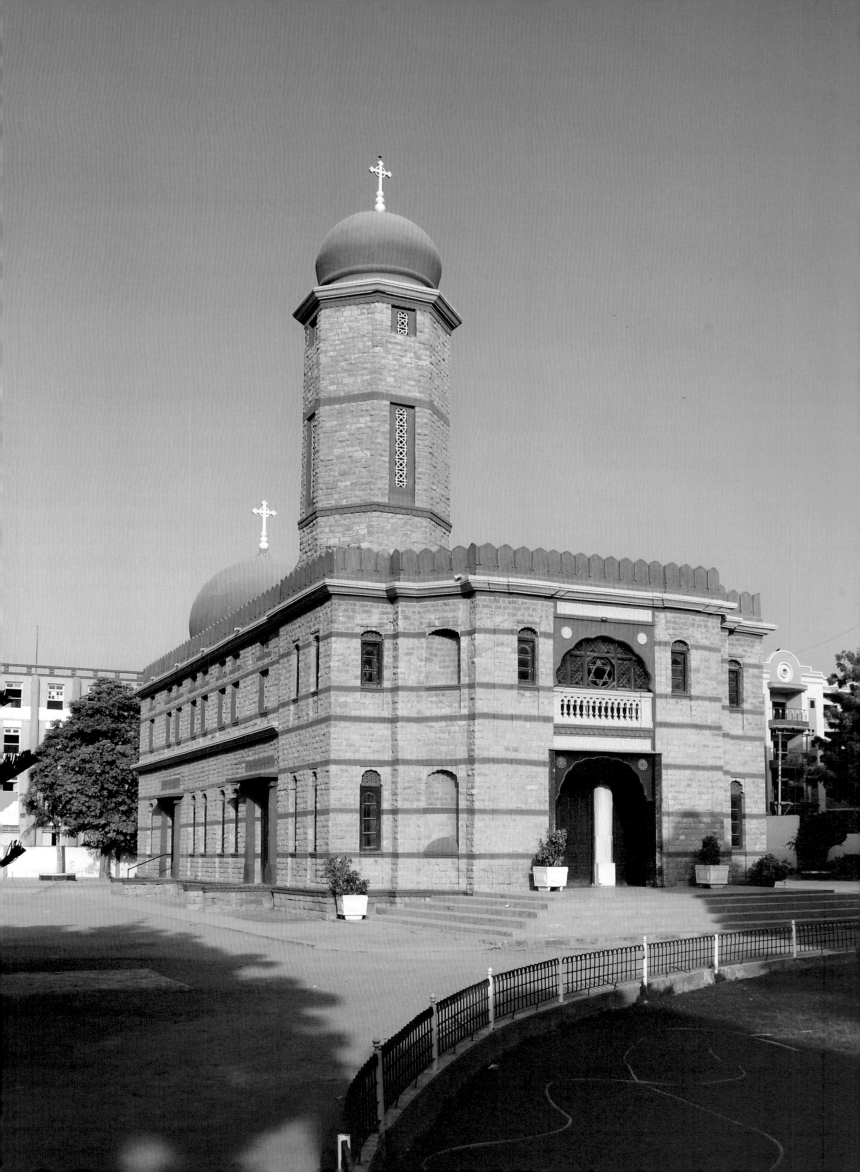

Festivities in St. Lawrence Church, Karachi.

Original woodwork.

The glittering altar.

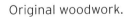 Built in the Mughal style, St. Lawrence Church celebrated its jubilee in 1981. The Jubilee Commemoration Plaque was blessed by His Holiness Pope John Paul II, on February 16, 1981 during his visit to Karachi, (Pakistan).

PROTECTED HERITAGE

GOVERNMENT OF SINDH

Holy Trinity Cathedral, Karachi is an elegant edifice unifying various church styles to suit the local climate. It was consecrated on March 18, 1855. The Cathedral is a protected heritage building and a marvelous monument of the city. The Father of the Nation and First Governor General of Pakistan, Muhammad Ali Jinnah, attended a special dominion service on Sunday evening after the Independence (August 14, 1947).

Holy Trinity was the garrison church. Soldiers and sailors stationed in Karachi attended the compulsory church parade every Sunday.

The monument in front was erected in 1849 by Sir C. J. Napier G. C. B. It is sacred to the memory of the soldiers of Her Majesty's 22nd Regiment of Foot, who died from the effects of climate in Sindh between 1842 and 1843.

WHILE THEY BEHELD HE WAS TAKEN UP

MARY HATH CHOSEN THAT GOOD PART

THY BROTHER SHALL RISE AGAIN

S·LUKE·X·42

S·JOHN·XI·23

TO THE GLORY OF GOD AND IN MEMOR

DIED 3RD JUNE 1878 AGED 31

Baptismal font.

Intricate decorative designs still retain their original elegance.

Stained glass in the Holy Trinity Cathedral, Karachi is a fine specimen of late Victorian glasswork.

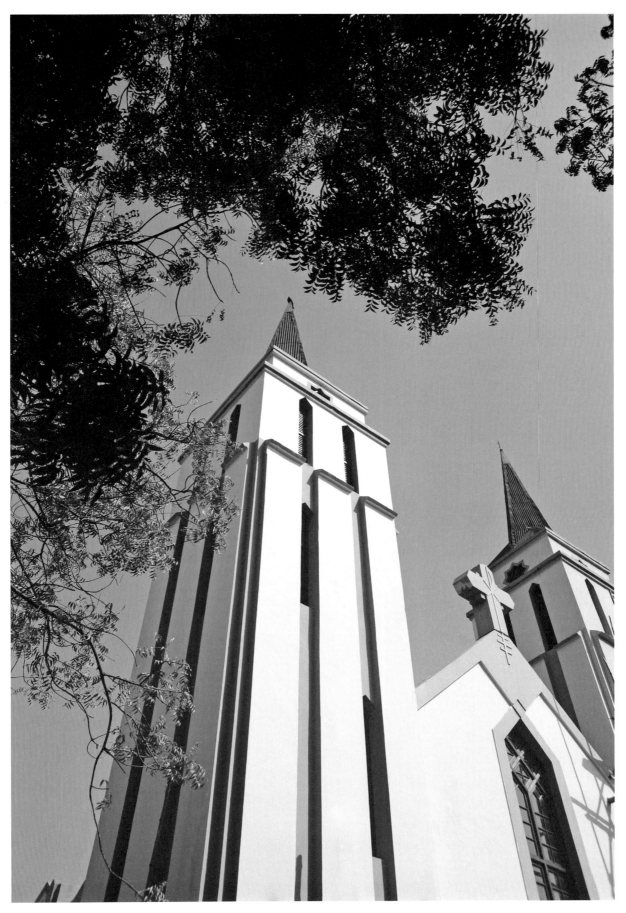

The elegant towers of St. Anthony's Church, Karachi, built in 1937. The Church serves as a mini shrine of the Archdiocese where devotion to Mary and the Patron Saint are regularly held.

St. Paul's Church at Manora Island in Karachi bay was built in 1885 for the sailors and their families. It was erected as a memorial to Sir John Napier who captured the Island in 1839. The lighthouse was inaugurated on April 1, 1889. Its beacon is visible up to 20 nautical miles.

Christ Church Mission High School, Karachi: Father of the Nation, Muhammad Ali Jinnah, was a student at this school.

Brooks Memorial Church, Karachi was built in 1875. ▶

Bishops of the Catholic Church in Pakistan

1. **His Grace Most Rev. Evarist Pinto**

   Archbishop of Karachi

2. **His Grace Most Rev. Lawrence Saldanha**

   Archbishop of Lahore

3. **His Lordship Bishop. Sebastian Francis Shaw, OFM**

   Auxiliary Bishop of Lahore

4. **His Lordship Most Rev. Maximus Rodrigues**

   Bishop of Hyderabad

5. **His Lordship Bishop Victor Gnanapragasam, OMI**

   Bishop of Quetta

6. **His Lordship Most Rev. Andrew Francis**

   Bishop of Multan

7. **His Lordship Most Rev. Joseph Coutts**

   Bishop of Faisalabad

8. **His Lordship Most Rev. Rufin Anthony**

   Bishop of Islamabad-Rawalpindi

Bishops of the Church of Pakistan

1. **The Right Rev. Samuel Azariah**

    Moderator, Church of Pakistan

    Bishop of Raiwind

2. **The Right Rev. Dr. Alexander John Malik,** Sitara-i-Imtiaz & Bar

    Bishop of Lahore

3. **Rev. Irfan Jameel**

    Adujator Lahore

4. **The Right Rev. Samuel Sant Masih Pervaiz**

    Bishop of Sialkot

5. **The Right Rev. John Samuel**

    Bishop of Faisalabad

6. **The Right Rev. Raffique Masih**

    Bishop of Hyderabad

7. **The Right Rev. Saddiq Daniel**

    Bishop of Karachi

8. **The Right Rev. Humphrey S. Peters**

    Bishop of Peshawar